The Ultimate

finding the

ED YOUNG

Copyright © 2000 by Edwin B. Young. All rights reserved. Written permission must be secured by the author to use or reproduce any part of this book, except for occasional page copying for personal study or brief quotations in critical reviews or articles.

All Scripture quotations, unless otherwise noted, are taken from The Holy Bible, New International Version (North American Edition), copyright © 1973, 1978, 1984 by the International Bible Society. Used by permission of Zondervan Publishing House.

Any emphases or parenthetical comments within Scripture are the authors' own.

Library of Congress Control Number: 2001092907

ISBN : 1-58695-012-6

Author: Edwin B. Young

Published by HeartSpring Media for On Purpose Media.

P.O. Box 1891 • Keller, Texas 76244
Toll free (877) 33 TAPES

Printed in USA – First Printing June 2001

Edited by Cliff McNeely
Layout and production by Russell Lake

CONTENTS

Chapter 1 1

Pre-Nuptial Nursery Rhymes
Moving from Fanciful Rhyme to Biblical Reason

Chapter 2 45

The Ulti-Mate Ride
Fixing the Flaws of Defective Dating

Chapter 3 83

Checks and Balances
Reading and Heeding the Relational Warning Signs

Pre-Nuptial Nursery Rhymes
Moving from Fanciful Rhyme to Biblical Reason

1.

My mother loves nursery rhymes. Name any of the big ones, *Old King Cole, Jack Sprat, There Was An Old Woman Who Lived In A Shoe,* and she can recite them right off the top of her head. During the first 48 months of my life, she repeated these nursery rhymes to me over and over again, before bedtime, naptime, mealtime, any time. As a kid, I bought into these rhymes. However, as I matured, I came to the realization that these rhymes were made up, orchestrated by someone with a very creative mind.

I don't have any illusions when reading about a political figure named Old King Cole. I don't think that I will ever be driving down a freeway and look to my left and see an old woman who lived in a shoe. They are phony, false, just for children. However, many of us are still reciting nursery rhymes and believing them. Men and woman in the throws of premarital bliss say Pre-Nuptial Nursery Rhymes as they walk down the carpeted aisle in holy matrimony.

Before I jump on that train and get more into the rhymes we believe, let me throttle back a little bit and share a couple of facts with you. A recent USA Today poll reveals that 49% of adults in America today are not married; they are currently single. Eighteen percent of those who are currently single have never been married, 15% are divorced or separated, and the rest are either widowed or living with a partner. It's clear that a lot of singles out there are looking for their ulti-mate, but too many of them are running into failure and disappointment. According to the latest study from the federal government, more than two-fifths (43%) of first marriages end in either divorce or separation within 15 years.

Many marriages today are not lasting because couples are not doing the work they need to do before they reach the altar. Singles need to understand the fine art of spouse selection. God's resources for a lasting marriage begin long before you say "I do."

Next to the decision to follow Christ, your choice of whom you will marry is the most important earthly decision you will ever make. And the best way to enhance your marriage for the long haul is to do the necessary work before the wedding day.

As I share with you these Pre-Nuptial Nursery Rhymes, I want you to think about how these impact life and relationships. Whether you're a single adult searching for the ulti-mate, a student who is just in the "going out" phase of life, or a single or married parent thinking about the future of your children, you need to understand the vicious cycle of fanciful rhymes that many of us have learned and continue to recite in our relationships.

The media encourages us to repeat these rhymes. Pressure from our culture causes us to do it. But, make no mistake, these nursery rhymes are not just innocent kid's stuff. They will mess you up. My desire in this chapter, and this book, is that you will take a step back and understand the reality of marriage and how high the stakes are before you make this critical decision.

The Hickory, Dickory, Dock Dance

Let's look at the first nursery rhyme that we repeat:

Pre-Nuptial Nursery Rhymes

> *Hickory, dickory, dock, the mouse ran up the clock; the clock struck one, the mouse ran down, hickory, dickory, dock.*

Hickory, Dickory, Dock! The old biological clock begins to tick, drowning out reason and common sense for both men and women. Women just want those little ones, the maternal instinct. And men would love to have a chip-off-the-old-block, someone they could throw a football with. And it causes us to be like the proverbial mouse. We become all freaky and frenzied about the ticking of the clock, run down the carpeted aisle and get hooked up. We get married just for the sake of getting married, without really considering whether or not we're marrying the right person.

Peer Pressure Cooker

This pressure to do the Hickory, Dickory, Dock dance starts when we are little kids playing dress-up with Ken and Barbie. It intensifies as people begin to ask us to be involved in their weddings, as a groomsman or a bridesmaid. Giddy girls rush up to us, their ring finger at eye level, showing us their relational rock. Friends ask them, "Oh, how did he ask you?" or "How many carats is that?" And a subtle form of competition begins. We don't really talk about this competitive urge, but turning over and over on the rotisserie grills of our minds are thoughts of beating the next person to the altar, of having a bigger ring, and of having an even more romantic proposal story for our friends to "ooh" and "awe" over.

With the increasing pressure to marry, singles begin to feel that married people are glaring at them. They imagine that they are singing songs to them under their breath, like "What's wrong with you, what's wrong with you, life will have no meaning until you say, 'I do.'" They find themselves at wedding receptions trying to get that elusive garter or the bouquet. They see themselves as an unclaimed piece of luggage at the airport.

You would think that parents would identify, that they

could relate. But parents drop these subtle hints, more like bombs. "When are we going to have a daughter-in-law?" "I really would like to have some grandchildren running around the house. You know, we are not getting any younger." Parents should not do this, yet they do. And it causes singles and students to say, "Hickory, dickory, dock, the mouse ran up the clock, and I am going to run down the wedding runner. I have got to get married."

The Time Factor

But the relational rush has a bad track record. Kansas State University conducted a study that showed a direct correlation between the length of a courtship and marital satisfaction. Dating is a lease with an option to buy, and most leases run for several years. That is why I challenge you to wait at least a year before you get married.

Our twins are learning to read and they pronounce every syllable, every letter. Take a hint from them. Singles, go s – l – o – w. The **TIME** factor is large. "**T**" stands for temperament. Date someone long enough to see his or her true temperament. What's their temper like? How do they handle stress and conflict? "**I**" stands for integrity. We get the word integer from integrity, which means a whole number. During a quick courtship too many of us are just giving out fractions, putting our best foot forward and only revealing our best side. With time comes knowledge of the whole person and all of their sides, good, bad and ugly. "**M**" is for maturity. Is this person mature? I'm not talking about chronological age but real growth and maturity. Are they ready for the responsibility and commitment of marriage? "**E**" represents enjoyment. Does this relationship put wind in your sail? Is this individual a friend? Do you really enjoy spending time talking to them and sharing activities together?

Six Months to Life

"Well, Ed, what if I wait too long? What if I burn up a year and then get married and discover that I could have gotten married six months earlier. I've wasted time." No, you haven't. Who cares that you dated the person you end up marrying a few months longer? This is a much better scenario than getting married six months too soon to the wrong person and regretting it the rest of your life. Six additional months of anticipation is a small price to pay when compared to a potential lifetime of regret. ==Please honor God's covenant of marriage enough to give it some time. Let the shine wear off and go s – l – o – w.== Don't do the Hickory, Dickory, Dock dance, because a rodent-like mentality does not work in marriage.

Humpty Dumpty Thinking

Pre-Nuptial Nursery Rhyme number two goes like this:

Humpty Dumpty sat on a wall. Humpty Dumpty had a great fall. All the king's horses and all the king's men couldn't put Humpty together again.

Are you a Humpty Dumper? Humpty Dumpty found out that it isn't easy being oval. Humpty Dumpters have this line of thinking, "If I get married, get hooked up with this special someone, they can fix my fractured life. They can put a cast around me and heal my brokenness." Record numbers of us are emerging from homes where there is some real broken-

Pre-Nuptial Nursery Rhymes

ness: alcoholism, drug addiction, abuse situations. You look at a person emerging from a family of origin like that and they are, oftentimes, obsessed and in a frenzy to get married. They think that the other person can do what all the king's horses and all the king's men cannot do: "They can fix me. They can heal me. They can make me whole. They can bandage me." Wrong.

The only person I know who is qualified to heal someone's brokenness is maybe Billy Graham, and he has been married about fifty years. Gary Smalley and James Dobson are also married. So don't get into this pipedream mentality that surely that special someone can do it for you.

Inspecting for Cracks

I will never forget what happened when Lisa and I bought a home. We found a fourteen-year-old place and fell in love with it. Before we went to the mortgage company to put some money down and sign the stack of loan papers, we paid for an inspection. And since we were buying the house directly from the owner, we accompanied the inspector to the house. When I walked in the front door, I saw the owners, the sellers, sitting on the hearth in the family room. I thought that was odd. I decided that they were being nice and giving us operating room to look around and see if everything was A-OK. I try to see the best in people. I'm a positive person.

The inspector looked around and saw a couple of little things broken and messed up, but that was about it. We bought the house and were thrilled with our purchase. The day we moved in I was helping the movers with some fireplace equipment and happened to put my foot on the hearth. To my horror the whole thing just split open. I don't want to name names, but, apparently, they were covering up the crack in the mortar.

Dating, if you don't date very long, is unrealistic. We put on our best clothes, our best cologne and perfume. We are on our best behavior with our best manners. We go to the best restaurants and the best movies. We always defer to one another, and we have that kind of mushy, puppy love for one another. This is not the real world. Those first few months of dating are a fantasy world, an unrealistic la-la land of superficialities and misleading sensations. Both parties are sitting on cracked mortar, trying desperately to cover up fractures.

When people mistakenly think that this dating scenario is the real world, they end up marrying someone without really knowing them. And then after two or three months or two or three years they realize, "Wow, my spouse was sitting on some cracked mortar in their lives before we got married. They are broken. They are messed up." If they had dated long enough to take a good look at the hearth, they might have seen the cracks.

Dealing with the Brokenness

When this realization comes (before or after marriage), when you begin to see pockets of brokenness, don't freak out. Don't say, "I am out of here. I am bolting." None of us is perfect; we all have fractures and cracked mortar in our lives. If you take the time, though, to discover the brokenness while dating, you can call on a trusted Christian friend or a Christian counselor to process the brokenness before hooking up in marriage. Don't do the Humpty Dumpty deal and expect that your marriage partner is going to fix everything after you get married. Do the work now and move into marriage as two whole people who have already dealt with the shattered pieces of your past.

The Jack 'n Jill Tumble

Here's another Pre-Nuptial Nursery Rhyme people often recite:

> *Jack and Jill went up the hill to fetch a pail of water. Jack fell down and broke his crown and Jill came tumbling after.*

A lot of Jack and Jillers say to themselves, "You know, if I get married, I will never, ever deal with isolation again. I will never, ever have a companionship yearning or be lonely again. For the rest of my life, I'll have someone to fetch pails of water with. Even if I fall and break my crown, I'll have someone to come tumbling after me. We are going to become just like Jack and Jill and that will be it. All of my companionship yearnings will be solved."

Filling the God Gap

To a degree, it is right to expect your spouse to fill your companionship longings. But on another level, it is wrong. We have two basic levels of compatibility yearnings.

The first one is the one I will call level A, and most of us are aware of this level. This level can be quenched, satisfied, through a deep friendship or a marriage. It is the yearning we have to be in community with another human being. We are wired for human relationships; God gives us this desire and that is a good thing.

However, there is a level B yearning that many of us don't realize is actually there. There is a God gap in our lives, a hole punctured in our hearts from birth that can only be filled through a personal connection with the Lord.

A Recipe for Disappointment

Here is what happens. You put ingredient A, our

human companionship yearnings, into the same pot with ingredient B, our God-gap companionship yearnings. Then you do the Julia Child thing and mix it up real well, or maybe you do the Martha Stewart thing with the very expensive bowl and spoon. And when you have A and B converging, you suddenly have a double desire to get married. You think this human being can solve both level A and level B yearnings. Since you may not be aware of the level B yearnings or how to quench them, you put unrealistic expectations on the person you are marrying.

So one day you find yourselves in a church and the pastor is looking at you saying, "Having pledged your faith in and love to each other, having sealed your solemn and significant vows by the giving and receiving of these rings, acting by the authority given to me by the State and looking to heaven for divine sanction, I now pronounce you husband and wife in the presence of God and these assembled witnesses. What God has joined together, let no man separate."

The nursery rhyme runs through your mind and you think to yourself, I will never deal with companionship yearnings again. Say what? Little does your new spouse know that, oftentimes, you are putting level B expectations on his or her shoulders. You are trying to get them to meet needs in your life only God can meet. A human being can't fill the God gap. I can't do that for Lisa. She can't do that for me.

A Futile Effort for Change

When we become disappointed and disillusioned with our spouse's ability to meet our every need, we take our spouse and try to tweak them. We try to change them, mold them, and make them into what we think we need, inching them and nudging them into something they are not. That doesn't work, and we wake up one day with even more problems. Jack sees another Jill and he likes the way she walks up that hill and fetches her pail of water. He leaves, gets a divorce, and goes to this other person. Jill sees another Jack and tumbles down the hill after him.

The vicious cycle begins of divorce after divorce, until one day you look in the rear view mirror of life and see all of this relational wreckage. You have damaged your life, and maybe two or three other lives in the process. If there are children involved, you have messed them up too. Why? You didn't understand level B, the hole in our heart that only Christ can fill. Don't get caught in the Jack and Jill tumble. It is a fairy tale fallacy resulting in disappointment and failure.

The Marital Stream

Here's a Pre-Nuptial Nursery Rhyme that will, no

doubt, sound very familiar to you:

> *"Row, row, row your boat gently down the stream. Merrily, merrily, merrily, merrily, life is but a dream."*

But you may not have heard this rendition: "Row, row, row your boat gently down the marital stream. Merrily, merrily, merrily, merrily, marriage will be a dream." It's dreamy, all right. But you'd better be prepared for some bad dreams and an occasional nightmare. Yet I talk to people who tell me this, "When I get married, I will be complete and most of my problems will fade away. I am single and those problems are sticking to me now like Velcro, but, once I get married, no more of that junk. I'll live happily ever after with the white picket fence and 2.3 children."

It is so tempting to think this way. I know because I have said these rhymes before too. Marriage is great. It is a wonderful thing. But a character transformation is not going to take place the moment you step over the line in holy matrimony. Ladies, if he is a jerk prior to marriage, he is going to be a world class jerk after marriage. Hey guys, if she is a materialistic gold digger before marriage, she is going to be a major gold rush mama after marriage.

Look for those little red flags that are evident in every relationship, if you're paying attention. Those times when you think, "Oh, I don't like that" or "That kind of gets on my nerves." Those little dislikes and discomforts will turn into monstrous flags billowing in the breeze when you are married.

The Single Advantage

The Apostle Paul addressed this in 1 Corinthians 7. Before we look at this text, let me set the context. Any time you read a Scripture verse, don't just pick and choose. Always ask yourself what was the situation, what was going on around this passage? Paul was writing these letters to the church at Corinth. We have a lot in common with this very metropolitan, worldly city of Corinth. Some of the people in the church at Corinth who were unmarried had some serious problems. They were worshipping idols and getting drunk at the communion table, among other things. So Paul told them here that they need to think carefully about getting married and be aware of the special problems marriage might bring. They already had enough problems to deal with in their single lives, before adding the complexities and additional responsibilities of marriage.

That is the context of 1 Corinthians 7:28, "But those who marry will face many troubles in this life," -- the Living Bible says "extra problems." -- "and I want to spare you this." While most of us will get married at least once in our lifetime, God does give some individuals, a few of us, the gift of singleness. And it is a true gift.

The Matrimonial Reality

Throughout this book, you will feel a tension, a cross-pull, and let me tell you why. On one hand, the single life is a viable, biblical lifestyle. It is a good thing if you are not married. On the other hand, being married is a viable, biblical lifestyle. It is also a good thing. But understand this right up front and read about it in God's word: marriage has problems.

Think about financial problems. He wants to buy a new set of Calloway golf clubs and she wants a new sofa for the den. What about relational challenges? He wants to have his friends from college and their wives over, but she doesn't because all they talk about is sports. She wants to go out with some friends she met at church and their husbands, but he doesn't have anything in common with them.

And then there are the sexual problems. She was really feeling romantic last night, but he came in from work at 9:30. He is in the mood tonight, but she is tired and a little put out that he came home so late the night before. When the context of the relationship isn't right, she's not in the mood. He's often clueless about the context and doesn't understand why she's rebuffing his advances.

When you get married you have got to say, "I'm sorry," thousands of times. You have got to eat your words often and you have got to compromise, concede, and conciliate. And I haven't even mentioned what happens when children come into the picture. But I think you are getting the picture. I'm not trying to scare you away from marriage, but I want you to go into it, if you go into it, with eyes wide open.

Erasing the Scarlet Letter

It is time we take the word sin out of the word single. We think singles have this scarlet "S" on them. One of the major problems that I see with the evangelical churches across our country is that they cringe at the word "Single!"

But let's look at some biblical trivia. A lot of prophets in the Old Testament were what? Single. The Apostle Paul was…single. Jesus Christ, you know this one, was…single. Yet most churches today would reject these biblical personalities I just mentioned simply because they are…you guessed it, single. Where did we go wrong?

    At Fellowship Church we do not frown on hiring staff who are single. On the contrary, we believe that singles have a unique perspective, commitment and dedication to ministry that many who are married are unable to have. Don't discount your single days, or while them away until you are married. If you do, you'll be wasting the incredible opportunities for ministry you can have before the unique problems and responsibilities of marriage set in.

From Nursery Rhymes to Biblical Reason

Learn the Secret

If you are doing the Hickory, Dickory, Dock dance, here is your challenge. Learn the secret of Philippians 4:12, "I have learned the secret of being content in any and every situation, whether well fed or hungry, whether living in plenty or in want. I can do everything through him who gives me strength." Contentment is the tranquility of your soul, satisfaction with where you are and confidence in God for your future. Let me tell you something from experience. If you are not content as a single, you are not going to gain contentment the moment you get married. A relational rock on the ring finger of your left hand is not going to get you there.

Here is what the evil one wants you to do. The evil one wants you to so concentrate on what you do not have—I don't have my man...I don't have my girl...I don't have my dream home—that you miss your single shot and all the unique opportunities the single life can bring right now. You miss this incredible season when you can be scoring touchdowns, shooting three pointers, and knocking the ball out of the park for the glory of God while you are single. Incorporate the 4:12 secret into your life now, while you are single, and it will continue to serve you well when you are married.

Discover The Real Fix

Hey, Humpty Dumpter, you know who you are. Here is your word of advice in Psalm 147:3, "He heals the brokenhearted." "He" is not a spouse. We are talking about God here. Only He can fix your fracture and bind up your wounds. Allow the great physician to bandage you up, to heal you, to fix you. Don't sit on that hearth and try to cover up the cracks, hoping your potential mate won't notice.

Give Peace a Chance

If you're playing Jack and Jill on the hill, here is what

you need to do. Give peace a chance. I am not talking about some LSD-driven, John Lennon, Yoko Ono, Hare Krishna type trip. I am talking about the peace that surpasses all understanding, that only comes through a personal relationship with Christ. In John 14:27 Jesus says, "Peace I leave with you;" — it doesn't come from a spouse — "my peace I give you. I do not give to you as the world gives. Do not let your hearts be troubled and do not be afraid."

Join the Advantage Club

If you are row, row, rowing your boat up that marital stream, thinking that marriage is a dream, join the Advantage Club, The Single Advantage. Look again at I

Corinthians 7, verses 32-34, "I would like you to be free from concern. An unmarried man" — this includes unmarried women — "is concerned about the Lord's affairs, how he can please the Lord. But a married man is concerned about the affairs of this world, how he can please his wife, and his interests are divided."

Do you know what really fires me up? Thinking about the singles who are involved in the ministries of Fellowship Church. These people commit to three, maybe four, ministries because they have time. They are taking their single shots and taking advantage of this season of their lives. They are shooting three pointers, scoring touchdowns, knocking the ball out of the park for the glory of God. Our church is made up of almost 50% singles and we couldn't survive without them. And your church can't survive without singles either.

Also, if you are single and part of this Advantage Club, think about the friendship factor. You can have more and deeper relationships with others. You can have many more deep friendships than I can, because I am married and have four children. My time, energies, and priorities are more divided. You have a single shot in the Advantage Club. Enjoy it while you can.

In the Midst of Ministry

I was talking to my brother awhile back. Ben is a noted author and the only Christian singles-driven talk show host in the country. I'm going to give a shameless plug for his books, *The 10 Commandments of Dating* and *The One* (just released in 2001). Check them out. They are well worth the read. He is also a Singles Pastor in Houston and deals with hundreds of singles. He asked me, "Ed, do you know what the single biggest problem is that I deal with in my ministry to single adults?" I said, "What? Materialism? Pre-marital sex?" He responded, "No, none of those things. It is single adults who jump from church to church. It is church hopping, never plugging into the life and ministry of a local church."

Many singles are always looking for the hottest scene. "Oh, this church over here has it going on. I had better hang out here for awhile." "Wow. Look at the babes over there. I like that Jill. I like that Jack." Then they get tired of that, they've dated everyone they want to there, so they go to another church and check it out. What is so thrilling about Fellowship Church is that we have a core group of singles that are life-timers. They are engaged and involved, with roots that run deep into the life and ministry of the church.

Now, I am partial to Fellowship, but there are many

Pre-Nuptial Nursery Rhymes

great churches around. Don't float. Don't hop and bop. There is no such thing as a Christian floater in the Bible. Get hooked up to a local church, because—as you are involved in a local church, learning the secret of contentment, discovering the real fix, giving peace a chance, and joining the Advantage Club—one day you may look over to your right or to your left and lock eyes with your **Ulti-Mate**.

finding the love of your life

The Ulti-Mate Ride

Fixing the Flaws of Defective Dating

2.

It happens in the automotive industry with a striking regularity. Cars, trucks, vans, even SUVs are recalled because of defective parts. Recently it happened to me. I received this letter from the Ford Motor Company:

Dear Mr. Young,

This notice is sent to you in accordance with the requirements of the National Traffic and Motor Vehicles Safety Act. Ford Motor Company has decid-

> *ed that certain 1999 super duty F250 and F350
> trucks failed to conform to Federal motor vehicle
> safety standard no. 301. During fuel system integri-
> ty testing, fuel may leak at a higher rate than
> allowed by regulation. Call your dealer without
> delay. Ask for a service date and whether parts are
> in stock for safety recall 99F11.*

When I received this letter, I didn't ignore it. I got the problem fixed. A thinking person wouldn't even entertain the thought of ignoring a recall letter.

I want to address in this book something in many people's lives that is defective, something that needs to be recalled. It is not an automobile. It is something much more important than that. I'm talking about dating. Most of the dating that is done today is defective. Think about it. Would you drive a defective car? Would you tool around in a car that has a part that could endanger your life and the lives of others? Of course, your answer is, "No, that would be reckless and stupid." Yet, far too many of us date in a defective way, endangering our lives and the lives of others.

The majority of spouse selection going on today is skewed and needs to be recalled. You might be thinking at this point, "Ed, what a broad-brushed and generalized statement. Come on. You're telling me that more people than not are defective daters." Yes, it doesn't take a relational rocket scientist to see that we are messing up.

The United States of America leads the world in divorce. Of ten marriages that will occur this week, five will end in divorce. Of the five that endure, half will report little or no intimacy whatsoever. The average marriage lasts 9.4 years and, sadly, the children are caught in the crossfire. Sixty percent of children born today will spend some time in a single parent household.

Even the little ones are seeing that spouse selection is not working the way we are currently doing it. My family and I were seated around our kitchen table having dinner and EJ, our eight year old, said, "Mom, Dad, a friend of mine told me today that his parents are getting a divorce."

We said, "Oh, EJ, we are sorry. Show your friend a little extra care, be sensitive to him."

Then one of our twin daughters said, "Mommy, Daddy, will you guys ever get a divorce?"

Lisa said, "No."

Our daughter responded by saying, "Thank you. Thank you."

This issue of dating and spouse selection is important for everyone, because it impacts society at so many different levels. Maybe you have recently gone through a divorce and you are just stepping back into the dating scene. Maybe you are a 20-something, 30-something or 40-something single adult and you have never been married. Maybe you are a single parent. Maybe you are a student. Even if you are currently married and a parent, you need to pay attention to this issue, because the moment our children are born we are involved in an intense spouse selection process. We are mirroring to them how to choose their mate, whether we know it or not.

FLAWS OF DEFECTIVE DATING

I want to bring to light some flaws of defective dating.

And, hopefully, the exposure of these flaws will teach us what *to do* by making clear what *not* to do. To illustrate the various problems I am going to pinpoint, I want you to picture in your mind a Mercedes Benz convertible. That's right, a brand new, top of the line, pop-top Benz.

The Mercedes 500SL convertible is a dream car for a lot of people. Almost anyone, really, would not turn down a ride in this fine automobile. And I want you to keep a picture of the ultimate ride in your mind's eye, as we discuss God's ultimate in dating and selecting a mate.

Steering Deficit Disorder

The first flaw of defective daters is that they don't take enough time to see who's behind the wheel, the person who is driving the relationship. If you don't see who is behind the wheel, you have a great chance of messing up on one of the most important decisions you'll every make: choosing the person you will marry.

Do you know what the Bible says? The Bible says that the person behind the wheel has towering implications on the relationship, in dating, in marriage and later in the challenges of child-rearing. The Scripture tells us that Christ-followers should only date and marry other Christians, true believers. In other words, we should make sure that Jesus Christ has the keys.

Well, how do you do that? How do you know that your date or potential mate is a true believer? A true believer always has a how-I-gave-Christ-the-keys story. And they should be able and willing to share with you what kind of driving Christ has been doing in their life since the key transfer. If someone does not have that story, they are not a believer. They are not a Christ-follower. Even if they have known about Christ since they were a child, they should still be able to articulate how they gave their life to Christ and what that means to them now. If someone says, "I've always been a Christian," watch out. If someone says, "My parents were Christians and I grew up in church," watch out. These statements do not reflect a personal decision of giving one's self to Christ, of transferring the keys to Him.

This is the most fatal flaw that I see on the dating scene among Christians today. Too many are compromising their most fundamental beliefs by getting intimately involved with non-believers. I cannot stress strongly enough that you are inviting disaster when you do this. You may not see the storm clouds right away, but watch the horizon. The storms will come and they will be devastating.

The Bible shares with us a highly unpopular text in 2

Corinthians 6:14, "Do not be yoked together with unbelievers. For what do righteousness and wickedness have in common? Or what fellowship can light have with darkness?"

When singles read this text you would think they would say, "Okay, God is the creator of marriage and surely He knows the best way to select a spouse. I am going to do it God's way." Most singles shake their head because this verse eliminates a large amount of potential prospects. And singles, when they read this, say, "Wait a minute! It is hard enough to find someone who is sane and healthy. Now they have to be a believer, too? That's pretty heavy."

Some see this word yoke and they say, "Yoke, what a

joke. Aren't egg yokes supposed to be bad for you anyway? I am an egg white guy. I am an egg white girl." This yoke metaphor is something we need to grasp. A yoke is simply a wooden contraption that goes around the neck of animals and is tethered to a plow. If animals were equally yoked, for example, oxen of equal strength, then the farmer could plow the fields in straight lines. If he had one animal that was stronger than the other, an ox on steroids compared to an ox that was lame, the yoke and the plow and the farmer and this whole process would be directionless.

If we want to have a great marriage, we have got to be equally connected. Jesus Christ must be driving the vehicle. He must be driving our vehicle and the vehicle of the person we are considering hooking up with. Don't date nonbelievers because you can fall in love with a nonbeliever. And, if you do, you will never reach your full potential.

At this point, some single women begin to tell rational lies to themselves. They say, "Oh, I am going to take my unbelieving hottie and I am going to win him to the Lord. He will say a little prayer and get a little baptized, be a part of the little church and everything will cruise. This freeway is going to be so smooth…"

Ladies, let me tell you something about guys, because I am one. They will do anything, say anything, get baptized any way just to be with you. You cannot trust a hormone-driven decision while you are dating this person. If you are dating someone and this someone is not a believer, back off. Don't date him. Then watch and see what happens. If he becomes a Christ-follower, if he grows and Jesus becomes fully formed in his life over the next year or two or three, then think about dating. But not any time before that. Now and then it happens the other way around, with the guy thinking he can change the gal, but nine times out of ten women get caught in this trap.

God Knows Your Ulti-Mate Destination

I am a why person, always asking why. Why would

God set forth these standards? Is God being restrictive? No. God is being protective and He wants the best for you and the best for me. That is why I picked a Mercedes 500SL, a $90,000 sports car, as an illustration. This is one of the best cars made. But in God's economy, your life and mine make this incredible car look like a wreck. That's how much we are loved and the kind of potential we have. God wants to spare us the pain and agony of being unequally yoked, of being hooked up with another human being who does not have the same strength, the same octane or the same RPMs that Christ brings. Why? God wants us to be equally yoked with believers because His desire for us is that we reach our ulti-mate destination.

That is what dating is all about: to find the ulti-mate. I don't care how casual it is. I don't care how flippant it is. Down deep, I'm talking even to guys now, you are thinking, "Could she be the one? Could she be my wife, the mother of my children? Could I grow old with her?" And I know, women, that you are thinking the same kinds of thoughts about the men you date. Do you want to reach your ulti-mate destination? Do you want to hit on all eight cylinders? Then Connect with another Christ-follower. Frankly, my heart is grieved and broken for so many people who make the wrong call, thinking they can somehow reach their ulti-mate destination without being equally yoked. It is a formula for failure.

God Has the Owners Manual

Another reason why God insists on us being equally yoked is that He wants you and me to read from the same owner's manual. The Benz has an owner's manual, and part of the owner's manual deals with trouble shooting issues. I have heard rumors that, in marriage, conflict can occur. Some arguments can occur. The marital equation is pretty basic: one sinner plus another sinner equals double depravity. And the Bible tells me that the moment I receive Christ into my life, He gives me the ministry of reconciliation.

That means that when I do something wrong against

my lovely wife, Lisa, the Holy Spirit begins to work on me, to nudge me and to say, "Ed, Jesus died on the cross for you and rose again. You don't deserve it, but He did it. And He forgives you and took the initiative to reconcile you to God. Do the same to your wife." When those marital troubles hit, we both have the ministry of reconciliation and we reconcile. If you are not using the same owner's manual, you are in serious trouble. It is just a matter of time before your marriage is broken and banged up and becomes wreckage on the relational road.

God Charted the Parent Map

Another reason why God insists on this compatibility

issue is that He wants us to study the same parent map. Most of us, when we get married, will have children. Child rearing is challenging. My wife and I have four children. It is one of the most difficult but rewarding things that we do. I cannot even think about trying to parent without a unified front. I couldn't even imagine trying to parent my children with Lisa driving one way and me going another way. We read and study the same parent map. We have these values, these transcendent truths given to us from God, and we teach those to our children. They are also reinforced in the church.

    Don't you see the genius of God? He is not being

restrictive; He is being protective. He wants the best for you and the best for me. Too many of us, though, are caught up in superficial distractions and never look at the most important thing. Is the person you are dating, considering as a mate, truly a Christ-follower?

The Showroom Mentality

Another flaw of defective dating is what I call the showroom mentality. Talk to car dealers and they will tell you about the 24-hour principle. They will tell you that when American men and women think about buying a car, walk into the showroom, look at the lines and focus on a few features of the car, most of them will drive away with the car in the first 24 to 48 hours. They make a quick decision based on just a few features. That is the showroom floor mentality. How many American men and women focus on just a couple of superficial features without thinking about the whole car? How many people consider marriage without reading the maintenance record, the warranty, Consumer Reports? How many make the second most important choice of their life, aside from their relationship with Christ, based on incomplete and faulty facts?

Marital statistics bear out that too many of us have and continue to make these mistakes. I could roll you tape after tape of conversations, tell you about many sad situations, of people who have this showroom floor mentality. Romance is important. Feeling that feeling is important. But your relationship cannot be built on romance. And one day your children will ask you this question, "How do I know if he or she is the one?" And most of the time parents just smile and answer, "You will just know."

No, that is not good enough. You just know? Are we going to buy into this Hollywood-style, quiver-in-your-liver definition of love? "I have got to feel this romantic, erotic stuff. And when I feel that, when we lock eyes, it is just a slam-dunk, a no-brainer. We are in love." It doesn't work that way.

Fleeting Love

There are two types of love. Eros is that erotic, obsessive, mysterious aspect of love. It has got to be there. God has given us the chemistry, the desire for the opposite sex. That is a good thing. Your potential spouse should be someone you are attracted to. Your heart should beat fast when you see this person. But I will tell you one more time. A relationship cannot be built on eros alone, because eros usually only lasts nine months to a year.

I remember the first year in my relationship with Lisa. It was eros driven, romance driven. I wanted to be with her every second of every day. But I dated her long enough to let the eros, the passionate romantic love fall into its proper place. Romance has to be ruled within the context of the total relationship. Too many times we focus on a few features. We feel that romance stuff going on and we take off down the aisle. Push the clock forward three years, we wake up one Saturday morning, the eros has faded, and we look at our spouse and wonder, "Who are you?"

Lasting Love

There is another kind of love. Agape love is that commitment-based love. It is that nurturing and companionship love. Any great relationship must be built on agape and, when it is, when that is the foundation, eros love will ebb and flow. Lisa and I have built our marriage on agape and it has gotten stronger and stronger. Because of that foundation of lasting love, the eros part has also grown and flourished. But, too often, students, single parents, those who are playing the dating game, those who have been recently divorced, get duped into thinking that "feeling it" means they have found "the one."

One of my favorite verses of Scripture is I Samuel 16:7. Here is what God told Samuel. "The Lord does not look at the things man looks at. Man looks at the outward appearance but the Lord looks at the heart." We need to do the same thing. The passion must be there but it is a heart issue, not a couple of outward, superficial features. Are you a defective dater who needs to pay attention to the recall notice and say, "You know what? I've been involved in this showroom floor mentality. I need to change."

Off-Road Hazards

A third flaw of defective dating involves the off-road hazards of sexuality. You will not hear this talked about in the church very much. The church has messed up royally on this one, because it has not articulated clearly enough what I am going to address here.

What if I just took the keys to a Mercedes 500SL and gave them to you. What if I said, "You are a great girl or guy. I want to give you this $90,000, eight cylinder Mercedes convertible. Here you go." You know what you would say? "Man, Ed is my favorite person. I just love that guy." And I will tell you what you would also do. If you received those keys, you would take care of the car. You would garage it. You would wash it. You would park it by itself to keep it from getting door dings. And you would drive this very expensive car where it is supposed to be driven—on the road. You would not take it off road.

Yet, too many times we take this gift of sex given to

us by God, this Mercedes Benz, this desire that is to be practiced on God's freeway, on His Autobahn, between His guardrails, and use it in a God-forbidden way. We jump in the back seat, we put a ramp right next to God's guardrail, rev up the engines like Robby Knievel and we go off road. This car has been built, tested, and approved for city and highway travel. It does not have four-wheel drive and is not meant for joyriding through field and stream. Mud would get all over the place and cloud your vision. The car would get stuck and the more you pressed the accelerator, the deeper it would sink. That's what happens when we do sex our way instead of God's way.

"Oh, yeah. Right, God. You created sex. You are pro-sex. You have told me five times directly and twenty-three times indirectly to abstain from sex until marriage. But you know, God, I know more than You know about this. I am just going to go off road, because I would rather experience the thrills and chills of sex than do what I should be doing in dating: building communication, working through conflict resolution, and understanding if we are spiritually and emotionally compatible."

This off road mentality is why record numbers of people marry the wrong person. It is the power of sex. Sex blinds us. It is a multi-faceted practice, impacting us physically, spiritually, psychologically, and emotionally. Mud gets all over us and the more we get involved, the more we press the accelerator, the deeper we sink. We look over at this person and we can't tell if he or she is right for us or not. And we fall in lust, not in love, and marry them.

Recognizing the Biblical Guardrails

Paul wrote something regarding sexuality to a group of people in the first century with whom, I believe, we can identify today. The Thessalonians lived in a very sexually saturated culture. Extramarital sex was applauded. In some of the Greek religions of their day it was called an act of worship, believe it or not. And don't think we have one up on them, that they were barbarians and we are somehow above that kind of depravity. All you have to do is channel surf, surf the net, or just live life to see the bombardment of degrading sexual images and ideas that permeate our culture. The world does a God-ordained thing in a God-forbidden way. But, obviously, their way is not working.

In 1 Thessalonians 4:3-5 Paul tells the Thessalonian church, "It is God's will that you should be sanctified,"—the word sanctification simply means more dedicated to God—"that you should avoid sexual immorality, that each of you should learn to control your own body in a way that is holy and honorable, not in passionate lust like the heathen who do not know God." The Bible gives several Biblical boundaries regarding sex. The first word the Bible uses is *adultery*. Adultery is when a married person engages in sexual activity with someone other than their spouse. The next word is *fornication*. Fornication means having sex before marriage. The third concept is **sexual immorality**. That is a general term which includes everything up to the point of sexual intercourse.

You may have thought, as do many others, "I cannot have sexual intercourse until I get married, but I guess God gives me the green light to do everything else up until that point." I hate to rain on your sexual party, but God's design for sex relates more than just to actual sexual intercourse. There are basically three gears that pastors, theologians and counselors have pinpointed regarding a physical relationship with someone prior to marriage.

The first gear is the kissing and the hugging stage. The second gear is the caressing stage, or sensual contact with your clothes on. The third gear is the stimulation stage, genital contact that often leads to climax. Sexual immorality occurs when you go into the second and third gear.

This heavy sexual activity just short of intercourse can cause guilt, separation and alienation in the relationship. You are committing sexual immorality when you do those things, and you are damaging the relationship. God's plan, God's standard, for sex is designed to bring unity and closeness in the relationship, not alienation and guilt. Only within the context of a committed marriage before God can we truly experience all aspects of sex in the way God intended.

On the Road Again

Well, you may say, "Ed, I have messed up sexually. My virginity is past tense." Or maybe you are "technically" a virgin but have lived in third gear for a long time. "You mean, Ed, that I should stop at first gear? I am sexually experienced. I can't stop." Oh, yes you can. I have a close friend in Houston who was very promiscuous before he became a

Christ follower. Then he gave his life and his sexuality to the Lord. A few years later he met a beautiful young woman and he stayed in first gear for a year until his wedding night. And he will tell you that God did great things for him in that area of his life. He shared with me a couple of years ago, "Ed, I have been with a lot of women. I know that God has forgiven it and forgotten it, but I wish I had saved myself for my spouse."

If you haven't lost your virginity, don't. Give your spouse the ultimate gift on your wedding night. If you have, God will forgive you. He will cleanse you. He can remake you and remold you. So stop having sex until you get married and God will truly bless that area in your life. Don't you see, again, that God wants the best for us? He doesn't want us to trash His gift. He doesn't want us to go off road. He doesn't want us to make a poor decision based on the power of sex.

Maybe you are thinking, "You know, Ed, this whole defective dating deal is a picture of me. Talk about not looking behind the wheel, that's me. Talk about showroom floor mentality, that's me. Talk about going off road, that's me." Come to the Lord and He will fix the flaw; He can change a defective part, if you'll just pay attention to the recall notification.

In the next chapter, we'll look at another flaw of defective dating. Defective daters will look at the car and check it out, but they fail to pop the trunk. It's hard to look at what's in the trunk, the baggage that all of us carry. This baggage blunder is a big one and actually leads to three other dating flaws.

Checks and Balances
Reading and Heeding the Relational Warning Signs

5.

In this chapter, we're going to look at four more flaws of defective dating. All of these involve, to one extent or another, checks and balances in the relationship that are being neglected or ignored. If you're paying attention to the warning signs, the road signs, the red flags, the cargo in the trunk, you're in good shape. This means you are engaged in the relationship with your eyes wide open and your radar at full scan. But, sadly, many people date and enter serious relationships wearing side-blinders. They get caught up in the superficial aspects of dating and are simply not paying attention to the deeper, lasting issues that need to be examined in a long-term commitment. God wants you to use your common sense and good judgment when considering a commitment like marriage, and you've got to clue into the checks and balances He provides along the way in order to truly find your ulti-mate.

Bags 'N Baggage

Defective daters will look at the car and check it out, but they fail to pop the trunk and examine the luggage. Who can blame them? It's hard to look at the emotional, spiritual, and relational baggage that all of us carry. This baggage blunder can lead to all sorts of other problems and, in particular, we'll look at three other dating flaws that stem from baggage neglect.

Ladies, I know your hottie seems so perfect right now, so unbelievable, but in reality he is Samsonite Sam, loaded down with suitcases. Guys, I know that babe you have your eye on, that girl that you have been dating, looks like the ulti-mate. She could be the one, but she is also Louis Vitton Linda, weighted down with a bunch of baggage. Before you say "I do," you'd better look in the trunk, on the luggage rack, and inside the loaded down U-Haul trailer that some people pull behind them.

Let me reiterate, once again, that we all are loaded down with luggage. Baggage doesn't really cause problems, unless we pretend like we don't have it or unless we are unwilling to process it. The blunder comes not from the existence of baggage but from ignorance and neglect.

The Family Duffel

The first bag is called the family duffel bag. People who do spouse selection God's way will really check out the family situation. Why? Because the family dynamic wields the most power, it has the most influence, on who you are and who I am. That is where our self-esteem was formed and our value system was learned. We, for the most part, understood what marriage is all about and what church life is all about from our upbringing. The family formula is major, so make sure you take some time out of your busy dating schedules to open the family duffel and look through the contents. You must have intentional conversations related to your family's high points and low points.

It is also important to deal with the family bag, because it is the bag that causes a lot of dings and scratches and dents in our lives. No one comes from his or her original family unscathed. No one emerges from imperfect parents looking like a brand new Mercedes Benz. Even those coming from the best of families are still banged and bruised a little bit. Your parents were imperfect. My parents were not perfect. And our parent's parents weren't perfect either.

So many in today's society grow up into Blaming Boomers or Generation Excusers, who love to say that they are the way they are because their mother put their diapers on too tight or the nursery was painted the wrong color. They blame, whine and claim they are the victims. For the most part our parents did the best they could at that time, and it's time to take responsibility for ourselves and say, "You know what, this is my family. I am who I am. It is time to deal with the baggage." So make sure you talk about it.

Romans 3:10 is a great baggage verse. It says, "There is no one righteous, not even one." In other words, we all have baggage called sin. Sin is imperfection or missing God's mark. Sin loads every individual and family down and causes lots of cargo carnage. The key is how we deal with the carnage in our lives, both past and present. Ignoring it is not the solution. Wise spouse selectors open the trunk and carefully inspect the family bag. They also make their own family duffel available for a thorough search. Like an airport security agent searching a bag, you need to keep your eyes open for potential problems and then deal openly and honestly with them—before you get married, not after.

The Temperament Carry-on

Spouse selectors also need to open another bag: the temperament carry-on. Each of us is wired in a unique way, just like different machines are wired in unique ways. For example, the Mercedes 500SL is wired much differently than a Ford F250 pickup truck. Because you are wired differently than the person you are dating, you had better talk about the wiring challenges. Maybe you are a planner and you have got to have everything organized just so. You can't function without your palm pilot or day-timer at your fingertips. On the other hand, the person that you have your eye on is a spontaneous, off the cuff, individual who likes to make it up as they go. They like to get behind the wheel, take a left turn or maybe go straight as the mood strikes them. They might even enjoy an unplanned day trip, but you prefer an ultra-planned weekend excursion. This is a wiring challenge that must be addressed.

Maybe you are a spender who likes go to the mall and shop till you drop. You like to take financial risk with investments, but the other person is much more conservative, playing it close to the vest. You have got to think about and talk about this difference. The temperament challenges are those day to day irritations that cause friction and create tension in marriage. Out of the blue the wife will look at her husband and say, "The way you chew ice drives me nuts." The husband will look at the wife and say, "The way you organize your shoes, honey, please, I can't take it anymore."

Conflicting Styles

You can't say the word temperament without saying the word "temper." This leads to the major issue of how we handle conflict, which is directly related to how our family of origin handled conflict. How did your mother or father, or your potential mate's parents, deal with car trouble, wrecks, problems along life's journey. Maybe you grew up in a family that handled conflict SWAT style, where the hurt party just started firing verbal shots at everyone else. You might have grown up in a family that handled conflict frappaccino style, where the standard response was to ice the other person out. Or perhaps your family handled conflict ziplock style, collecting the negative pain and anguish, cramming it into a ziplock bag and placing it in the refrigerator. It sits there for two or three months, until someone opens the refrigerator one day and POW!

I want to save you a lot of time and trouble about conflict resolution. I have been married for nineteen years and have gone through a number of different disagreements and arguments. I have boiled it down to this: almost all conflict is over PMS. Don't get mad at me. I am not referring to the PMS you are thinking about, ladies. I am talking about P, power issues. In the process of becoming "one flesh," the "I" fights for survival and neither person wants to give up personal control. M stands for money. Statistics bear out time and again that most of the marital mayhem we deal with is over finances. And then there is the big S, representing sexual issues. It is tough enough just to remain sexually pure until you get married, to stay on God's autobahn and not go off-road. Bet even after marriage, you will have sexual compatibility disagreements.

Well, the Bible has an answer for all conflicts both

prior to and within marriage, no matter what particular issues they stem from. God tells us in Ephesians 5:15 to speak the truth in love. Proverbs 15:1 says, "A gentle answer turns away wrath, but a harsh word stirs up anger." The Bible also says in Ephesians 4:26 that we should not let the sun set on our anger. You can count on one thing in any relationship: you are going to have conflict. Whether it's a power issue, a money issue, or a sexual issue, how you deal with conflict will be the saving grace in your dating relationship and in your marriage. Take time to find out about your potential mate's family conflict style and temperament, and then begin to discover together how God's guidelines and boundaries for conflict can bring healing, reconciliation, and greater intimacy in your relationship.

Dashboard Warnings

Something else that defective daters do is to ignore the dashboard warning lights and gauges. Maybe you have seen the dashboard of a Mercedes, resembling the cockpit of a 747. I am continually amazed by all of the dashboard warning lights, buzzers and voices that communicate with us in the computerized vehicles we drive today. Sometimes these technological bells and whistles get on our nerves, but they are designed to warn us and protect us.

One day I was tooling around in my truck and I noticed that the fuel gauge had been on full for the last three days. At the time I was driving a Ford F250, 4 x 4, that drinks fuel so fast I can almost watch the fuel gauge go down while I'm driving. I knew the gas tank could not still be full, so I decided that it was broken and I probably needed gas. I pulled into a service station and put in $41 worth of fuel. For three days I was just into the trip, not really paying attention to my fuel gauge, until it was almost too late. If I hadn't noticed at the last minute that the gauge was stuck, I would have ended up stranded on the side of the road.

Many of us date in much the same way. We're not paying attention to the dashboard warnings, because we are just into the trip. "Oh, forget the warning lights. I don't need any gauges to tell me what to do." There are several warning lights, gauges and signals that you need to monitor in any serious relationship. Ignoring them is a recipe for disaster.

The Character Gauge

First of all, you need to monitor the character gauge of the person you are dating. I can't say this very often, but the political jargon of recent campaigns is right: it *is* all about character. Is this person responsible? Does this person have a high personal integrity value? Does this person have a consistency and a predictability in their personality and habits? Some say, "Well, you know, he just has a little gambling problem." This is a character problem. Are you watching the gauge? These "little problems" have a tendency to get bigger, blow up and cause relational wrecks once you get married. "Well, she has a little drinking and drug problem. It's really not that bad." Who are you trying to kid?

Ask yourself this question: Can I hang out with this person as my spouse for the next 20, 30, 40, 50 years and respect their character? Or how about this question: Do I want to have the same character that they have? These are tough questions that must be asked if you're serious about having a life-long, Christ-honoring relationship.

The Relational Rearview Mirror

Another indicator to look at is the relational rearview mirror. When you are trying to find the ulti-mate, you had better look at how they have handled relationships, past and present. Look in the rearview mirror of their lives and assess the relational history. Does he or she have long-term, nurturing friendships? Is he or she pretty square with their parents. Do they have a good reputation on the dating scene or have they left a string of relational wreckage behind them? If everything looks good, then that's great. But if it doesn't look good, if they have a short track record with relationships or problems with their parents, always bickering and arguing, you'd better pay attention.

The Maintenance Light

The next warning sign is the maintenance light, or, more appropriately, the high maintenance light. This one is costly, because it requires frequent tune-ups and service calls. If you look on your dashboard and see dollar signs flashing, if you pick up vibes about driving this car, living in this zip code, wearing only certain clothes, listen to my advice. Here is what you need to do: get out of the car, go to another dealership, and try out another car. You need to understand the BMW or Bangladesh theory. The person you marry must be equally satisfied if you are driving 17 BMWs or if God leads you to a mission opportunity in Bangladesh feeding the hungry. If they aren't, head for the hills.

When I think about Lisa, I am so glad I dated her long enough to see these issues play out. Lisa is a woman with an impeccable character, high integrity and morals. One of the reasons I married her is because she is so consistent. I never wonder how she will act, how she will process dealing with a family that is really poor or another family that has millions of dollars. I never wonder if she will be swayed by any of that. She never is.

I think about her relationships. I look back in her life and see people who love her and honor her, and I can see how Christ-centered her relationships are. Lisa is also low maintenance. She has never insisted on living in a certain house or neighborhood, driving a certain car, or wearing a certain label on her clothes." This speaks volumes about who she is as a person and how she relates to me as a husband.

Now, I am not saying that Lisa and I are perfect. We are just like you, fellow strugglers. But I am saying to you, and this is so important, that you have got to be very intentional about seeing and processing these dashboard warnings. And you have got to date long enough to really be able to see them with any clarity and honesty. Love is not blind, only temporarily impaired during the infatuation stage of the relationship. When the blinders of initial infatuation are taken off, these various warning signs will begin to hit you. And it is a far preferable scenario for them to appear before you are married than after. Also, don't ignore your family, your friends or others in your life who see warning signs that you are apt to miss. They have an objective perspective that you can't possibly have in the midst of the relationship.

The Test Drive Deception

Another defective dating habit involves taking this car illustration too far. The rationale of those who engage in this flaw goes something like this, "I'll take a test drive before I get married. Come on, I wouldn't walk into a dealer, plunk down $90,000 and take a Mercedes home without at least going through a test drive. So I think I should at least take my potential mate out for a little spin." This is a common rationale these days in dating, "I'll just cohabitate with the person, play a little house and try things out for a while before I seal the deal."

The logic sounds so good, and I understand why people would buy into it. Because so many adults are the products of broken homes, they don't want to go through that wreckage again with the person they marry. Some also say they do it for financial reasons or to see if the love is real.

Sex, No Pink Slip Required

People today are living together prior to marriage in record numbers. Let me tell you why people live together. Let's start with the reason men do it. Do you know why, ladies, guys are living with you? Two words: free sex. It is the best of both worlds for guys. They can glean the sexual benefits of marriage without the commitment. Do you remember in the movie *Grease* how guys would drag race for the pink slip, the certificate of title, of their opponent's car? Well, guys today are living with women so that they can have the sex without the legality, the official union, of marriage. Now some ladies might say, "Ed, you don't know my man. You don't know the man I am test-driving. Surely he is not living with me just for sex."

Well, if you don't believe me, let me give you some homework. Go to the apartment or house where you are doing the test drive, sit down at the kitchen table, look into his eyes and say this, "Baby, for the next two months we are not having sex." He'll be out of there in a couple of weeks. Ladies, men won't tell you this, but I want to save you some pain.

Marital Manipulation

Now, ladies, do you know why you test drive? It is

not because of sex. I know ladies enjoy that, but that's not it for them. It is because you think you can manipulate your man into marriage. Research reveals that over 70% of women who test-drive, who cohabitate, have marriage on their mind. And the other 30% are living in denial.

A survey done by The Houston Chronicle several years ago reported that women who lived with their man before marriage had an 80% higher chance of divorce than those ladies who did not live with their man. Washington State University did another study, revealing that ladies who test drive with their boyfriends are twice as likely to battle depression and to go through domestic violence than those who do not.

Hit the Brakes

If you are test-driving, let me give you a pastoral word. Do it God's way. Put the brakes on and move out to different residences. You can still date the person, but you have to wait for the sexual part until marriage. I would challenge you to let many, many months go by until you know you have saved yourself and are truly ready for marriage. Then when you know that the person is the one, have talked with a pastor and attended pre-marital counseling classes, you can walk down the wedding runner. God will bless that aspect of your relationship in a mighty and glorious way.

When I spoke on this subject in church, a couple that was test-driving took this challenge seriously and moved out until their marriage. When I spoke with them later, they urged me to highlight this point and emphasize how critical this move was to their future relationship together.

God's Relational Road Signs

Other signs along the way also need our attention. I call these relational road signs. And defective daters are notorious for disregarding and failing to observe these signs. On my way to church one Sunday, I stopped at a stop sign and a truck beside me just flew through it. Fortunately, this reckless behavior did not cause an accident. But if you don't observe the road signs of life, you have a high likelihood of getting into a serious relational wreck.

Speed Zone Ahead

The first sign that singles must observe is the Speed Limit sign. I say this often to singles in my church and will say it again here: go slow and get to know. Wait at least a year until you marry. Here is some great information, a 411, on taking it slow and being patient. I can tell you from experience that the more time that peels off the clock will cause you either to have more confidence or to erode your feelings concerning the vehicle of marriage. It is so important to wait and to evaluate your feelings and commitment, to both your potential mate and to marriage.

So many get married too young and too rapidly. A recent study by the federal government regarding women and marriage concluded that the older a woman is at first marriage, the longer that marriage is likely to last. Women who get married young are almost twice as likely to divorce than those who wait until their twenties and early thirties. Many relational experts believe that it is best for single adults to get married after they are 28 years of age. They assert that, because the period of adolescence is longer in modern times, most people are not mature enough until they are at least 25.

When I think about going slow, I think about Genesis 29 and Jacob's relationship with Rachel. Jacob met Rachel and he was immediately attracted to her; he knew he wanted to marry her. One day he kissed Rachel and afterwards just started weeping. You can read it for yourself. That must have been some kiss. Then Jacob asked Rachel's father for her hand in marriage. Rachel's father said that he could have her, but first he needed to work for him for seven years.

Genesis 29:20 says, "So Jacob served seven years to get Rachel, but they seemed like only a few days to him because of his love for her." I am going to direct my three daughters' future boyfriends to this text. When you consider Jacob's patience, a minimum of one year of dating and waiting for marriage is starting to sound pretty good, isn't it?

Don't Be Afraid to Stop

This next sign is going to take some guts to observe. It's the stop sign. I can't tell you what to do because I am not you. But if you have a check in your spirit, if you see some warning lights or some baggage that hasn't been dealt with, have the guts to stop. If it doesn't feel right, stop. "Well, Ed, the invitations have been sent out." Stop. "My friends are pressuring me." Stop. "He is rich." Stop. Don't be hesitant to do that, because you are talking about a decision for life, a forever commitment.

Make a U-Turn

Whenever you hear the term repent in the Bible, it means to do a U-Turn, to go the opposite way, to do a 180. I love this symbol, because it illustrates what God does. God tells me that when I just begin to turn, He is there to greet me, to save me and to change me. He doesn't wait for me to go all they way. No, He is meeting me by the curve of the U, and that gives me confidence. It should give you confidence too.

A lot of defective daters need to come clean and say, "I have messed up. I have a lot of dating flaws in my life. I want to do a U-Turn and begin to do this stuff God's way. I want to drive on His street, between His guardrails, and on His autobahn. I don't want to go off-road. I want to really understand and process this biblical perspective on spouse selection." Good for you. All you have got to do is begin to turn the car and God will be right there.

Yield the Right of Way

The yield sign is shaped like arms outstretched to God in a yielding position. That should be our posture before God. We become a Christian by saying, "God, have your way in my life. I receive Christ into my life." And we become an *effective* dater when we say, "God, take the right of way on this dating journey. I give all of my desire for the opposite sex and all of my baggage to you. I want to go Your way." When you do that, you will meet your **Ulti-Mate**. And it will be a lot better than driving a Mercedes 500SL.

Check out the many creative resources from Ed Young by logging on to www.OnPurposeMedia.com or call toll free (877) 33 TAPES.

lily santander.536yahoo.com

Lily Santander
770 843 7876
Maria delos Angeles